KRISTI,
MAY
BE HUG

That Man Is Dead

Dennis Otto
with Brian Scott

9FOOT
VOICE

www.9footvoice.com

9 Foot Voice - Minnesota

Cover design by Brittany Kalscheur
www.brittanykalscheur.com

ISBN: 978-1-951849-00-9

To my beautiful wife Patti,
for showing me how to love again.

To my dad and mom, Leo and Mary Ann Otto,
for never giving up on me.

To my brother-in-law, Matt Longawa,
for his boldness in Christ.

Contents

Forward

He was a monster of a man with his arms outstretched singing and praying to God. He stood up front, shadowed by the light from the band.

Amy nudged me. We had come in late and found a spot in the back. "That's Dennis," she said. "That guy up there is Dennis."

"The giant?"

She grinned and nodded. After worship he came straight for us, this guy with jeans and a collared shirt. Amy had given me the thirty-second synopsis of his life story. Ran with bikers. Cooked meth. Sentenced to ten years in prison. He smiled at me, and, as I shook his hand, I had a hard time believing any of it.

As we got to know each other, it seemed even more unreal. I'm a trauma surgeon but our friendship had nothing to do with his heart issues. God didn't need us connected from a medical standpoint. God needed us connected as spiritual men to build something new.

Dennis helped me through a transition in my life. I had a lot of garbage I had to work through, a life to rebuild, and this man with the big arms in church became a powerful tool of healing for me.

But that other man: the meth cook, the convict, the brawler; I barely knew he ever existed. Dennis rarely talked about that part of his past. It was hard to believe the man I knew - generous friend, mentor to my two sons, Nick and Jack, minister of the gospel - could have had anything to do with that other life.

In the trauma center, we are often looking for that impossible moment of resurrection. Everyone wants that miracle, but the reality is we see it only 1% of the time.

If we look at the way Christ works, however, he's raising people from the dead every day. The miracle everyone wants is open to all of us without ever stepping foot inside a hospital.

And it's the only way to explain Dennis. The meth cook, the tough guy on the motorcycle looking for a fight? That man is dead. Jesus performed a miracle in his life and raised up someone new.

It has been a blessing to get to know this new man in Christ. Dennis, the walking miracle, is now bringing the love of God wherever he goes. He's shining light in prisons, in halfway houses, among addicts, in families... and in this book.

- Tom Blee, MD
Creator and Co-Director of LIFEteam,
a hospital-based intervention program
Author of <u>How to Save a Surgeon</u>

GOD —
SAVES

One

"**D**ennis, where are you at, spiritually?"

I was at the end of the table, my usual place. Matt sat across from me. We had known each other for over a year but had hardly shared a word together. He didn't care for me much - and for good reason. I had recently done time in prison. I had a history of addiction. I had cooked and sold meth. I had been classified as a violent criminal.

And I was dating Matt's sister-in-law, Patti. I was in my fifties and nineteen years older than she was. Of course he was suspicious. The whole family had concerns about me. Any family would.

I understand it now, but it bothered me in the moment. I could feel the way they looked at me. I could tell what they were thinking.

And I resented it.

It didn't help that her whole family was very religious, which I considered childish. I had spent years in the world of addiction and prison. I'd seen too much to believe there was a God.

Still, Patti and I had a son together so I went to her family functions. I'd sit quietly at the edge of the group and focus on my food. Afterward, I'd complain to Patti on the ride home. "These Christians... they don't even know me, but they're judging me."

I dragged my feet to every get-together, but it was at one of these meals that everything changed.

We went to a restaurant to celebrate something, I didn't care what. I was there to do my duty as boyfriend and father, and nothing more. I greeted Patti's sisters and parents, then sat next to Kayden, my toddler son. I focused on him and did my best to ignore the family's laughter and joyful conversation. I ate my burger and tried to keep Kayden from fussing too much. As I finished my fries, I checked my watch to calculate how much time we had left. I was about to give Patti the look - let her know with my eyes it was time to go home - but I sensed something strange.

Matt was staring at me.

"Dennis," he said.

I looked up. He leaned into the table and without any warning he asked me that question.

Where was I, spiritually? It was an intimate thing to ask a man who was wiping ketchup from his fingers. My first response was anger. *You never talked to me all this time and that's what you say?*

I wanted to give him a zinger and went through several within a matter of seconds. They all pretty much came down to, *Don't you know who I am? Don't you know what I've done to people?*

I opened my mouth, but before I could say anything, I heard a voice.

Be honest.

I've done a lot of drugs in my life, but I'd never heard any kind of voice in my head before. It sounded real. I didn't know where it came from, but I had to close my mouth. I listened for a moment - this all lasted two or three seconds - but it had gone quiet.

I shrugged and went back to my zingers. But as I leaned forward to stare Matt down, the voice spoke again.

This time it sounded angry.

Dennis, for once in your life, BE HONEST!

My heart thumped painfully in my chest. I fought a quiet battle against my better judgment. Everything I'd learned from prison and the world of drugs screamed at me to shut up. But I decided for once to ignore it.

Through all this, Matt sat watching me with compassion. He looked ready to listen to whatever I was going to say.

I leaned back and shook my head.

I didn't know what was coming next, but it terrified me.

After decades of lies, I finally spoke the truth.

"Matt," I said, "I've been living in hell my whole life. I hope when I die it's better than this."

Two

Anyone can throw a punch. Anyone can sell a drug. Anyone can manufacture meth. None of it takes any special skill or strength or courage.

There is no glory in those stories.

This book is about what God has done. And about what God is doing. Look into the eyes of that man in my mugshot, and you'll see no life there. That man is dead. Now I'm alive.

Jesus still raises the dead.

And that's all that matters. Stories about guns and drugs and the gangster life might be exciting, but they only lead back to darkness.

Stories about Jesus lead us to the light.

Still, it is important to know something about me before I gave my life to Christ...

I was not a nice guy.

I was raised in a good Catholic home. I had loving parents. They had six children: two boys and four girls. Five became honest, hard-working people with families and good jobs.

One went a different way.

At thirteen I started stealing liquor out of my dad's supply in the basement. Even then, I wouldn't sip. I wouldn't stop at one.

I drank to get wasted.

At fifteen, I got caught breaking into a nearby country club looking for alcohol. Around that time I started smoking weed pretty much every day at school.

At seventeen, I somehow graduated and went to work in heavy construction. Every night I got drunk. On the weekends I did drugs. Then on Monday, no matter how messed up I'd been the night before, I showed up at the job site ready to go.

After one too many DUIs, I was court ordered into treatment for alcoholism. I showed up for the classes. I took them seriously. I stopped drinking.

But I kept doing drugs.

And my life only grew rougher.

I moved to the east side of St. Paul and started running with some bikers. They were members of a small club with a passion for fighting. Two of the guys had been kicked out of The Hell's Outcasts because they were too violent.

I fit right in.

We'd spend the weekends going to bars, waiting for someone to bump into one of us, waiting for a stranger to say something in the wrong tone of voice. Then it would be on.

I was good at what I did. I lost some, but I'd never back down.

Though I didn't join the gang, I worked with them to sell drugs for extra cash. I spent most of my evenings and weekends messed up.

Then every morning I'd drag myself out of bed and get to the job site.

In 1985, one of my best buddies beat a man to death over a drug deal gone wrong. He went down for murder one, and was sentenced to 35 years. A few months later my first son, Brandon, was born. I'd been living with his mom; both of us committed to this wild life.

One afternoon I remember holding my son in my arms. He weighed nothing. His eyes could barely open. He made a soft gurgling noise.

And I knew that was it.

I took the first opportunity to move out of the city. I married Brandon's mom. I eased off on the drugs and violence. Life quieted down, and for awhile I thought I had things figured out.

I liked my job. Eventually we bought a nice house. Soon my son, Ryan, was born. Then I had my daughter, Danica.

There's just something about having a daughter. If you've been the father of a little girl then you know what I'm talking about.

I thought I had it all.

Three

I was leaning back in the recliner, my now three-and-a-half-year-old daughter asleep on my lap. My wife sat down across from me.

"Dennis..." She fidgeted, nervous about something. "I asked Terry and Jan to come down on Friday."

I shifted gently towards her, careful not to wake my little girl.

She said, "I have something I need to tell you and I want them here for it."

Heat rose up into my chest and neck.

"It's Wednesday night," I said, "and I have to wait 'til Friday to find out?"

I knew it was something bad. Our marriage had soured over the past couple of years. She'd grown distant and would argue with me over any little thing. She had even started not coming home at night.

She shrugged and stared at the floor.

"What did you do?"

She didn't answer.

"Did you sleep with somebody?"

She shook her head. "It's worse than that."

"Worse than sleeping with somebody else?"

A commercial ended and the news came back on, but I no longer heard it. My brain was flexing, trying to figure it out. I came up blank.

My little girl kicked and her head slid from my shoulder to my elbow. I looked down at her, eyes squeezed shut, her mouth slightly open.

A terrible thought burst into my head. I looked from my daughter to my wife. The words barely came out.

"Is she mine?"

My wife bolted from the room before the last word was out of my mouth. The pain hit instantly. It would've hurt less if the house had collapsed on top of me. I broke down, huffing to catch my breath. Nearly blind from tears and rage, I was still able to gently get my daughter to her bed.

Then I left.

I drove immediately to northern Wisconsin, stopping only once for gas. I had a buddy up there who had been a state wrestling champ four years in a row. He was 6'4, almost 300 pounds. He was an animal.

I needed an animal. I needed someone big enough to babysit me so I didn't hurt someone or kill myself.

For a few days I raged around his house, jerking from moment to moment in a fury. But, as the weekend drew to an end, I started calming down until I found myself Sunday morning, sitting on his couch, back in my right mind. I thought clearly about my situation. It hurt, but I knew there was only one thing to do.

That afternoon, I drove home. I found my wife and asked her calmly to sit with me in the kitchen. She looked afraid as she took a chair.

I breathed deeply.

"If I kick you out," I said, "the ones who are going to suffer are the kids. But they didn't do anything. Our daughter didn't do anything wrong..." I had to close my eyes and take a moment. I believed this. Danica never stopped being my daughter. To this day and forever, I am still her dad.

"I'm going to swallow my pride. Now that I know what the problem is, let's work on it. Let's go to counseling."

Counseling didn't help. We went to our first session but didn't schedule a second. Before long, I found out she had another boyfriend.

I divorced her. She took the kids. I stayed in the house.

No building ever felt so empty.

Every night I'd pace around for hours until I broke down. Months went by like this. Finally, I told my boss to get me out of town. If I stayed in that house any longer I was going to go nuts. I was going to hurt somebody.

He sent me to Okoboji, Iowa. I drove down there half out of my mind with grief and hurt. My second night, I went out with a couple of the guys to a strip club. I stumbled through the door, looking for trouble. I slapped my money on the bar and shot back a glass of straight Jack Daniels.

It was my first drink in sixteen years. I always did drugs - I was basically a high-functioning addict my whole life - but I hadn't had alcohol since I was nineteen.

In that strip club outside of Okoboji, I drank hard. I quickly lost track of how many shots I had. Months of frustration and grief burned hotter inside me as the edges of the bar drifted out of focus. I gulped down more whiskey, and waited for something to happen.

Within a half an hour the bouncer was on the floor, his face a smear of red.

My friends pulled me off while I was still screaming nonsense. I shrugged them away and pounded out the door. For a few moments everything made sense. Someone hurt me so I hurt someone else. That was how it worked. That was how I coped. It was the only thing I understood.

I stumbled into the next bar. I slapped my money on the counter and took a shot. The ground heaved underneath me. Someone gave me the wrong look or moved the wrong way or said the wrong thing. Five minutes after I walked through the door, I was on top of a stranger.

There was a lot of blood.

As bad as that night was, it was only the beginning. When you don't know how to deal with pain, the pain never goes away. So I kept fighting.

After a few weeks, the police chief in Okoboji tried to talk sense into me. When he sat me down, he didn't call me Dennis. He called me by my new nickname, Psycho.

But I wasn't psycho. I understood what I was doing. I understood the consequences of my actions. I simply didn't care. None of it mattered. I hurt so bad I was hoping somebody would kill me.

I wanted to die.

I lost everything and didn't know how to deal with it. I had no coping skills, so for the next three years I dealt with my pain the only way I knew: drugs, violence and darkness. I saw bad things. I did bad things.

I was not a nice guy.

Four

"**D**ENNIS, where are you at, spiritually?"

It was the wrong question at the wrong time from the wrong person.

I had cooked and sold meth. I had power over other addicts which I regularly abused. I used violence to intimidate the people around me. I had been a liar and a thief.

Sitting in that restaurant with Patti's family, I had been out of prison for three years. I'd been sober for about six. But I was still living in the darkness.

I told myself I wasn't a bad guy. Life wasn't fair and I was just getting what was owed me. I did what anyone else would do if they had the guts.

I wallowed in the darkness and just kept lying to myself.

I'd probably be living that same lie today if Matt hadn't asked me that question.

"I've been living in hell my whole life," I said. "I hope when I die it's better than this."

These were the first honest words I'd spoken in years, and I figured they'd cost me. As they escaped my lips, I immediately braced for a sermon.

Matt nodded quietly, looking right at me. He seemed to be listening, but I'd been around Christians enough to know he was just waiting for an opportunity to preach.

When the moment came, however, all he did was ask another question.

"What do you think about God?"

"Matt," I told him, "the things I've done. The things I seen. Some of these guys - what they do in prison..." I shook my head at the memories running through my mind. "I mean... I seen a lot of stuff."

I went quiet for a moment. Matt didn't start in on how I was looking at everything wrong, or how I needed a positive attitude. He just listened.

"How can God let stuff like that go on?" I looked up at him. "Honestly, Matt, it's hard for me to believe that there is a God. I see good people, friends of my mom and dad, good people - they go to church all the time. But then I hear their little boy is dying of cancer or their daughter was hit and killed by a drunk driver." I shook my head. "Where's God? He's not helping people like that. And these are good people. If he's not watching out for them, why the hell would he do anything for a man like me?"

Even after that, the sermon didn't come. Instead, Matt asked me another question. I answered that one, and he asked me another. I was honest, surprising myself by sharing the truth about who I was, the kind of things I'd done. But no matter what I told him, he didn't seem to judge.

We kept on like that for an hour and a half. Everybody else left, even my girlfriend, Patti, but I barely noticed. Finally, I looked around at the empty table.

I grinned. "Looks like I lost my ride."

Matt drove me home, which gave us another half hour

in the car to follow the same pattern. He kept asking deeper questions and listened to my answers.

In the driveway, he put the car in park and turned towards me. Here, finally, was the big sell. I had been bracing for it for two hours, but all he did was ask one last question.

"Dennis, if I gave you a book, would you read it?"

I shrugged. I couldn't remember the last time I read a book, but after 50 years of acting tough, of hiding my pain, I had just poured my heart out to a man I barely knew. Clearly it was a night for new things. I told him I'd give it a look.

He handed me a copy of <u>One Heartbeat Away</u> by Mark Cahill. I turned it in my hands. It was short. I liked that.

I thanked Matt for the ride and the book, then stepped out into the cool night. I felt strange, exhausted but lighter.

Inside, Patti gave me a questioning look, but I didn't have much to say. I couldn't really put into words what had just happened. Besides, I had a book to read.

Cahill hooked me at the first page and I read until I fell asleep. The next day, as soon as I got home from work, I picked it up again. I kept going that night until I finished it.

It was a little after nine o'clock. Our son was asleep. The house was quiet. On the last page were two prayers. One, a prayer of salvation. The other, of condemnation. Don't go to sleep tonight, the author wrote, without praying the prayer of salvation. If you didn't, then by default you prayed the prayer of condemnation.

I fell to my knees. I knew the prayer of condemnation. I'd been praying it for fifty years. I'd been lying to myself and everyone else my whole life. I'd been living in hell, but I was done with it.

I wanted Jesus.

I closed my eyes in my living room and gave my life to

Christ.

Even as I prayed, I could feel everything change.

My whole life I had been missing something inside me - a hole in my spirit. I had tried to shove drugs and alcohol and violence and power into that hole, but nothing worked. I tried to act like I was okay, like I had everything together, but I was miserable.

For the first time in my life I didn't have to lie. Jesus filled in that hole in my spirit - and took care of the pain and garbage that went with it.

The next day when I woke up, I couldn't stop smiling. It was like my first day on earth. It was like I could see for the first time.

I called Matt as soon as I thought he'd be awake. He answered after a few rings.

I shouted into the phone. "I did it, Matt!"

There were a thousand things I could have been yelling about. Knowing my history, most of them were bad.

So Matt understandably took a quiet moment before he asked, "What did you do, Dennis?"

"Matt," I said, laughing. "I gave my life to Christ."

We celebrated like it was my birthday.

I was fifty-one years old on March 15th, 2010, at about 9:20 at night. But it was the moment my life began.

———— GOD ————
SHINES

Five

IN the first chapter of his gospel, John writes about Jesus, "The light shines in the darkness, and the darkness has not overcome it" (John 1:5).

For most of my life, all I knew was darkness. But then Jesus showed up.

The day after I gave my life to Christ, Matt drove me to the store. He wanted to buy me my first Bible.

We talked a few minutes, but I grew quiet as his truck rumbled through the suburban streets. It was a cold, gray day, but a warm light seemed to touch everything I could see.

Finally, Matt asked, "What are you thinking about, Dennis?"

I struggled to find the words. I had been a Christian for less than twenty-four hours, and I was having a hard time understanding what had happened.

I shook my head in wonder.

"It's like I'm seeing the world for the first time."

In the third chapter of John, Jesus tells Nicodemus, "No one can see the kingdom of God unless they are born again."

"How can someone be born when they are old?" Nicodemus asked (John 3:3-4).

He didn't get it, but as we drove towards the Christian bookstore, I was beginning to understand.

I was experiencing something new. It is called joy, and it is rooted in something beyond emotion, beyond how my day was going, beyond how I was feeling in the moment.

All I'd ever known was darkness. Now, through Jesus, I saw a world of light.

Six

For a few years - in the time after my first son was born and before our divorce - I thought I had life figured out.

I had stopped drinking. I only did hard drugs on the weekends, and only when we had a babysitter to watch the kids. I had a good job and became well known around town.

In Matthew 7:24-29, Jesus tells a story about a wise man who builds his house on a rock, where he had a good foundation. A foolish man built his house in the sand.

A storm came. The house built on the rock was fine. But the house built on the sand was blown away.

I thought I had built a good life, but it had all been built on sand.

The storm started after my ex-wife took the kids. I ran away to Okoboji but eventually came back in order to be a part of my children's lives. For awhile I kept things going by flipping my drug use. During the week, I'd numb myself with drugs. Then, on the weekends, when my kids would visit, I'd clean myself up.

It kept me sane enough to function.

But then the storm swept my house away.

I worked hard at being a good dad. I made sure to fill my home with love and warmth. Still, the other five days a week, my kids' heads were filled negative messages about me. They started showing up less and less on the weekends.

Finally, they stopped showing up at all. With them gone I had nothing. I had built my life on the wrong foundation, and it cost me everything.

I walked around in constant pain. I numbed myself with whatever I could find. It was bad, but it got a lot worse when a young man in a darkened garage introduced me to a methamphetamine called red phosphorous fluff.

I took it greedily. It was so pure, so clean, it rushed through my bloodstream and left me feeling strong, like I could take on the whole world by myself.

The effect on my life was immediate. I stopped working for the first time since I was seventeen. Instead, I stayed home to cook and sell red phosphorous fluff out of my garage. I started running with a motorcycle gang and hanging with strippers and drug dealers.

I leapt head first into the darkness.

I'd get high and stay up for three or four days at a time. I carried pistols wherever I went. I was a dangerous person, because I didn't care about anything.

I'd always had a temper. If I got hurt emotionally my instinct had always been to hurt somebody else because it made me feel better for a little while. But now, as a full-time drug dealer, violence became my life.

I'd start every day in my garage, cooking meth. In the afternoon I'd distribute it and collect the money. At night, I'd dump the cash into a casino.

My house was filled with addicts who would do anything for a fix. I had power and abused that power, but none of it meant anything to me.

I was cut off from my kids. I ended any real friendships I had. I shattered my relationships with my parents and siblings.

My life became hell. I didn't care about anything. I didn't care if I got pulled over. I didn't care if I went to jail. I didn't care if I got into a fight. Nobody could hurt me because inside I was already dead.

I walked around, carrying an image of toughness. My attitude told everyone if you mess with me I would kill you, but, deep down, I knew that wasn't who I truly was. Looking back, I know God never abandoned me. Through it all, I could hear his voice, trying to remind me something had gone wrong. I'd been created for something better.

It made me tired.

One night I stood in my backyard tending the chemical fire. I had a lot of material to burn because the police had been searching my garbage. My friend Kevin - he went by Opie at the time - stood next to me.

"I'm tired," I said. "I'm tired of living like this. I want out."

Opie laughed and poked at the fire.

"Dennis, men like you and me, we don't get out." He laughed again. "We die."

There was no point in arguing. He was right.

I was forty years old. I had nothing. I was nothing. All I had, all I knew, was darkness.

Seven

GOD shines light into darkness.

I'm familiar with both.

I've known the darkness better than anyone. And I now know the hope and power of Jesus' light.

When I was selling drugs, it wouldn't be unusual to have some serious cash on me at the end of the day, rolled up in a pocket. It had meant nothing to me. I spent most nights flushing it down a slot machine.

In contrast, the day after I gave myself to Christ I held my first Bible. It was nice. It had a leather cover. It was big and heavy. But it cost less than a hundred dollars.

The whole world might lust after the roll of bills, but to me, that first morning, nothing in the world seemed more precious than my Bible.

I thanked Matt a few times for the gift. He was quickly becoming my spiritual advisor, which he remains to this day.

I took that Bible home and opened it up to Matthew, chapter one. I read as Jesus spent time with the broken.

And healed the blind man.

And cast out demons.

I read how Jesus shined the light of God wherever He went.

Jesus had shined that same light into my darkness, and I saw myself clearly for the first time. I'd been broken and blind and filled with evil. But I wasn't that man anymore.

That man was dead.

As Jesus did for Lazarus in the Bible (John 11), He did for me. Jesus raised a dead man to life.

GOD
CONNECTS

Eight

SOMEONE gripped my arm. I spun around, my fist already clenched, immediately ready to lay out whoever I found. But all I saw was a sweet older lady, about a third my size, smiling up at me.

The woman ignored the look in my eyes and spread her arms for a hug. I stared at her, waiting for my heart to stop thumping in my throat.

I'd forgotten myself for a moment. This wasn't a prison yard. This wasn't a biker bar.

She kept smiling, as patient as a saint. There was no escape. She wrapped her frail arms around my back and brought me in for a hug.

This was church.

I'd been a Christian for about three days when Matt had again showed up, grinning in his truck. Our destination this time was something called Alpha at River Valley Assemblies of God in Apple Valley, Minnesota.

I knew nothing about this stuff. I grew up in a good home. My parents were Catholic. I did all the rites and we showed up on Sundays fairly regularly. But I hadn't been to church in decades.

And this was nothing like I remembered it.

Alpha is a program for people new to the faith. We were in a room filled with people excited to learn more about Jesus. Everyone was smiling. All these strangers seemed happy to see me. There was a lot of laughter and hugging.

I still don't like to be touched, so I tried to keep my distance, but within minutes I was wrapped up in the arms of a woman whose gray hair barely reached my chest.

As easy as that, I was connected. I ate dinner and listened to the program. By the end of the evening I had met dozens more people and even allowed a couple more to hug me.

I had known darkness could be contagious. It spreads through basements and garages, through the users and dealers caught up in the world of drugs.

I discovered that night, however, that light was contagious too. I was buzzing when I got home. I felt joyful. I felt alive. I felt full of the Spirit.

I felt like myself, like I was finally the person God had created me to be.

I was hooked. I showed up at River Valley for worship on Sunday morning. I loved the music and the message. Everywhere I looked, I saw Jesus. It didn't matter to anyone what I'd done. They knew my history, that I'd been a meth cook and a drug dealer. They knew I'd spent time in prison.

But still, they greeted me warmly and invited me to sit next to them.

God had connected me to this community. And I learned quickly that connection is the opposite of addiction.

Nine

WHEN I sold drugs, I was at the top of my little garbage heap in southeast Minnesota. Other addicts wanted to be near me. Each bedroom in my house had someone staying in it almost every night. I was surrounded by people, but I had never been more alone.

When you sink into addiction, the first thing you do is disconnect from anyone who truly cares for you. Your addiction cuts you off from family and community, so nothing is in your way as you turn more and more into yourself.

I cut off my family. I had no real friendships. I saw other people only for what they could do for me. And that's how they all saw me.

Bill was the kind of friend I had in that life. He was a tweaker, like me, and one day he pulled me aside to ask a favor.

"I got a buddy who just got an insurance settlement. He's hoping to make some quick cash with the money and was looking to get an ounce of dope from you."

I agreed, not knowing that almost everything he said was a lie. Bill's son, also an addict, had met a guy in a bar looking to buy an ounce. Since I wasn't dumb enough to sell that much meth to a stranger, Bill had made up the story.

Bill rode with me to a Perkins in Golden Valley. The parking lot sat next to the interstate, so there were big sound barriers across the frontage road. There was only one way in and one way out.

The buyer's truck idled under a streetlight. Bill stayed back as I climbed out to make the deal.

The man looked steady. He had the cash. I gave him the ounce of dope.

"It's a go," he said.

I thought I heard him wrong. "What was that?"

He didn't need to respond as thirty cops swarmed around me. An older lady near the entrance was a cop. A man standing at the bus stop was a cop. They came out of parked cars. They appeared from behind the building. Cruisers blocked the exits.

They threw me to the ground before I fully understood what had happened. An officer pointed an M16 at my head.

I didn't resist but heard a cop shout, "Put the gun down!"

Instantly, I knew what had happened. Bill didn't mean to set me up. He trusted his son who trusted a stranger in a bar. He sat in my truck, oblivious to the action.

Bill, being a tweaker, started going through my stuff as soon as I stepped outside. I had bought a new pistol earlier that day and had stored it in the center compartment between the seats.

He found my gun and was looking at it, trying to decide if I'd notice it missing.

I laid there with my life in his hands. The officer with the gun to my head had his finger on the trigger. If Bill made a stupid move, I was dead.

Bill dropped the gun and I was taken to the police department instead of the morgue, but this is what addiction looks like. It cuts you off from anyone who loves you. It separates you from family, from community, from God. It draws you away from all the things that make life beautiful until there's nothing left.

Ten

THE opposite of addiction is connection.

Since the beginning, God has taken broken people and connected them into something bigger and better than themselves.

Moses killed a man and ran away from responsibility. But God found him in the desert and connected him to his people. Moses followed God and became Israel's greatest prophet (Exodus 1-20).

Naomi lost her husband, her sons, and had given herself completely to despair. But God connected her to Ruth, who gave her hope and family (Ruth 1-4).

Mary Magdalene was all alone. Seven demons possessed her. Her life was a living hell. But Jesus healed her and connected her to the early Christian community where she became the first witness to the resurrection (Mark 16:9).

And Saul persecuted the early church until God knocked him off his horse and made him blind. In the dirt he was rebuked by Jesus for his sins. But then Jesus connected him to Ananais and the Christians in Damascus. He eventually became history's greatest evangelist (Acts 9).

God connects us. He did it in the Bible. He did it to me.

After I'd been worshipping at River Valley a couple of months, one of the pastors, Jeff Kerr, asked me to tell my story on video for a sermon series he was doing. He was preaching on Psalm 103: *As far as the east is from the west, so far has he removed our transgressions from us.*

A few days later I sat down in front of a camera and spoke honestly about all the things I had done, and what Jesus had done for me. Later, my story was broadcast to all the campuses. After that Sunday, I could barely walk across the parking lot.

"Thank you so much!" a woman would say. "Would you talk to my brother?" Or a man would ask, "Could you help my son?"

It wasn't long before Dave Phillips, another pastor at River Valley, invited me to join his prison ministry team. It all happened fast, but that's God. He plugged me into a Christian community and into a ministry. He put me to work, helping broken men, addicted men, find their way to Jesus.

I was connected.

God

Reconciles

Eleven

THE cardiologist knocked on the door. My sisters stopped laughing, and my dad scooted himself up on the bed. A grin - he'd been teasing the nurse - lingered on his face.

"Leo," the cardiologist said. "You're good to go home."

Dad had a minor heart attack two days before. For the first twenty-four hours he drifted, barely conscious, but that morning he'd woken up. He kept growing stronger, physically and emotionally, as the day went on until that night when he seemed to be fully back with us.

The cardiologist smiled. "We'll adjust your medication, but you can go first thing tomorrow morning."

It was great news and we celebrated as a family. But it was also late in the day, and I had some things I had to take care of at home. Since I'd see the old man in the morning, I said good-bye.

I squeezed my mom's shoulder and turned to my dad. He was an old German and not a hugger. I don't ever remember a kiss from him my whole life.

I can't say where it came from, but I leaned forward and gave my dad a kiss on the lips. It stunned him, I think.

It stunned me too.

As I walked out the door, I thought to myself, "That was really weird."

Still, I was happy as I drove home. The day before I thought my dad was facing the end. Now, it looked like we would have more time.

But my phone rang early the next morning and part of me knew before I answered. My sister's voice cracked as she said my name.

Dad had an aneurysm during the night. He never woke up.

The doctor had been right, in a way. It had been time for my dad to go home.

Twelve

AFTER the shock had worn off, and after I had time to work through my grief, I began to see how deeply Jesus had blessed me that night.

Too many guys I know lost their parents when they were in prison. Their fathers and mothers only got to see the darkness. But for me, after fifty years of causing them heartache, they were able to see the good in me.

Six months before he died, I was able to tell my dad I'd given my life to Christ. Full of light for the first time in my life, I shared with him about my church, and the things I was doing for Jesus.

He never responded much. He'd nod or grunt, but didn't talk about it beyond that. It discouraged me for awhile, until my aunt took me aside at a family gathering.

"I don't know what you did to him," she said, "but your faith and your church is all he ever talks about."

Connection is the opposite of addiction - and God had connected me to my father.

I am so grateful that God gave me that gift, that I could show my dad how I had changed. He and my mother never gave up hope. They believed in me even when I was at my worst. They saw good in me even when there wasn't any.

Two weeks before my forty-eighth birthday, I walked out of prison. I didn't want to go to a halfway house because I was sober and needed to stay away from addicts. I had no friends. I had no money. I had no place to stay.

My parents took me in, even though my dad had serious reservations. He knew as well as anyone what I had become. He knew I was violent. I was dangerous. I was a drug dealer.

And he was right to be concerned. When I moved in with them, I wanted to stay sober, but I also needed to make my money back. I faced twelve months of Intense Supervised Release. During that time I had to check in daily. My case worker knew exactly where I was going at all times, and would even follow me to make sure. There was nothing I could do in ISR, but as soon as it ended, I planned to start cooking meth again.

I wanted to be a sober drug dealer. That, I figured, was where the money was.

But something happened during those twelve months. God started making connections in my life even before I gave my life to him.

My dad was a good father, but like most men of his generation, he was a provider first. I grew up in a loving home, but my dad trusted my mom to raise the kids. His priority was bringing home a paycheck.

Because he was always at work, we never developed much of a relationship. When I moved back after prison, however, we had no choice but to spend time together. He was retired. And I wasn't allowed to leave the house except for work and AA meetings.

Like me, my dad worked construction his whole life, but his back and knees didn't work as well as they used to, so he had some projects around the house that he could no longer do. During the day, I tore the steps off his deck and put in sonic tubes.

As I worked, he stood nearby. We talked. About the work. About the day. About whatever.

My dad had a back room in his house. There were no TVs, no cell phones, no noise. In the evenings, he'd sit in the rocker and I'd be in the recliner. We'd listen to the wind push against the house. We'd watch the squirrels.

We talked. About the Twins. About the news. About whatever.

A month before the end of my probation, I started buying stuff for my new place. A friend had offered rental property. We had never discussed my moving out, but one morning my dad found me in the kitchen eating breakfast. He took the chair next to me and watched me quietly for a few minutes.

"Dennis," he said. His voice was softer than I'd ever heard it. "You don't have to leave, Son. We have plenty of room."

I looked at him, a lump growing in my throat. I had moved in as an ex-con. In my heart, I had still been a drug dealer. I was a dangerous man and my dad wasn't sure if it was a good idea to have me at home. But God had made it so everything changed. I finally knew my father and he knew me.

I was grateful beyond words, and part of me would have loved to stay with him and Mom, but I was almost fifty years old. I needed my own space.

I thanked him, but shook my head.

My new relationship with my father changed me. As I packed up my stuff, I no longer had any plans to go back to cooking or selling drugs. I couldn't imagine living that life any more.

I couldn't do that to my dad.

Thirteen

IF you are a father, you really cannot overestimate the importance of your relationship with your children.

The good news of my story is it's never too late. I was forty-nine years old when my relationship with my father changed me.

I try hard to live this with my sons. I tore something in my shoulder years ago. The doctor told me it needed to be replaced, but I kept postponing the surgery. My son, Noah, came up to me recently and asked me to play catch.

Of course I said yes, and we went out to the front yard. My older son, Kayden, came out to join us.

It was a beautiful summer night, but I was in trouble after the first throw. It started as a twinge, but grew worse until I almost started crying from the pain.

My wife, Patti, could see my face and yelled from the house, "Quit playing!"

I shook my head and tossed another one to my son. I don't have many memories of playing with my father growing up, but the ones I do have all involve catch. So I thought to myself, "I'm going to play catch with my sons even if it kills me."

I want to make sure I connect with my children.

Because our Heavenly Father wants to connect with us.

Because the opposite of addiction is connection.

Because Jesus connects us to the people around us.

Because you cannot overestimate the importance of the relationship between fathers and sons.

And because there is nothing better than watching my kid light up when he catches a pop fly.

GOD ——
ABIDES

Fourteen

Patti and I had been married for four years. We had two sons. We owned a house. I was active in my church. I had a good job, making good money for my family. When I could, in the hours between work and spending time with my kids, I did some ministry.

On December 3rd, 2014, I came home from a dentist appointment. After walking through the door, I immediately started gathering the gear I needed to go ice fishing. The house was quiet. Kayden, our oldest, was in school. Patti was with Noah, my younger son, running errands.

I piled the equipment in the truck. I hurried to the bedroom to change clothes, then returned downstairs. I grabbed my boots from the closet and sat down. I felt fine. I was excited to get to the lake, but when I bent over to pull on my socks, it felt like something snapped. A searing pain tore through my chest, up my neck and into my face.

The pain fogged my thinking, but I tried to dismiss it. I decided I was experiencing a delayed reaction to novocaine and figured it would quickly pass. I still wanted to get fishing.

Another wave of pain crashed over me, and I knew I was

in trouble. I wrestled my phone out of my pocket and dialed the 'nine,' and the 'one,' but stopped. I was alone and could barely move, but everyone knows tough guys don't call 911.

For a few minutes, I tried to sit perfectly still. I kept expecting the pain to ease up, but if anything, it grew a little worse. I hovered my thumb over the last 'one.'

I didn't want to die from stubbornness.

I leaned back in the chair, and struggled to breathe. This was something serious. I finally acknowledged I needed help, but in the same moment I remembered the front door was locked.

For the first time, I felt real panic. If I called emergency services, the EMTs would have to break my door.

The effort nearly killed me, but I managed to stand up. With my knees wobbling underneath me, I forced myself towards the deadbolt. The first step went fine. I had it under control. The second was a little shaky. My body weighed a thousand pounds more than it had that morning, but I didn't worry about it. At the third step, however, my legs gave out and I collapsed to the floor.

Laying on the ground, I had to finally admit this wasn't just a reaction to the novocaine. With an angry grunt, I hit the other 'one.'

Between gasping breaths, I explained my situation to the dispatcher. She told me that help was on the way. Satisfied, I hung up the phone and started crawling.

I didn't know if I was going to live through the day but I'd do everything in my power to make sure my front door would. It was the longest ten feet I ever had to move, but I unlocked the deadbolt a few minutes before I heard the sirens. Knowing I had done all I could, I rested against the wall to wait.

———

Twenty minutes later, an EMT was smiling down at me. "Well, Dennis," she said, "you didn't have a heart attack."

I nodded. The pain had eased back soon after they arrived. They had attached wires for an EKG, but hadn't moved me yet.

"That's great. Then I'm going to go ice fishing."

"Whoa," she said. "You may not have had a heart attack but clearly something serious happened. You need to come to the hospital."

I shook my head. "You don't understand. I need to get to the lake. They are biting. Here..." I pulled out my phone. "You gotta see some pictures of the fish I caught yesterday."

"I'll take your word for it. But you have to get checked out by a doctor."

"It was probably just gas."

She leaned back on her heels and raised an eyebrow.

"Let me ask you this: why are you sitting on the floor?"

I hesitated. I knew it was a trap and tried to think around it. But finally I told the truth.

"I guess my legs gave out."

"Dennis, you need to go to the hospital and get this checked out."

Still, I hesitated. I argued with the EMT, downplaying what happened until Patti and Noah came home. At that point I decided to go to the hospital because my wife gave me no other choice.

It turned out to be the right call. My blood pressure plummeted in the ambulance. At the hospital, they rushed me in for a CT scan. Soon after, a doctor hurried to my bed.

"Dennis, we need to get you to the University of Minnesota."

His voice was deadly serious and the look on his face was grim.

"Doc, give it to me straight. What am I looking at?"

"The main artery out of your heart has split in your abdomen. It's called an aortic dissection and you need immediate emergency surgery," he said. "It's serious, but if you can make it to the University Hospital, you'll have a fighting chance."

He said I had a chance, but his body language told me I was already dead.

The helicopter wasn't available so they raced me over in the ambulance. I stared out at the blue December sky as we rolled down the highway. The EMT guys sat quietly, not saying much. I figured they were waiting for me to die.

I started talking to God.

"Dear Jesus," I said, "this is your plan. This is your deal, and I accept it. If you want me to come home, let's go." I thought of Patti and my children. "I'll have some questions, but I trust your word. You said you watch over the widows and the orphans and I'll hold you to your word."

I took a deep breath. "But if you want me to stay, I will stay. And I'll serve you however I can."

A few minutes later, we arrived at the University Hospital. A team surrounded me before I was off the ambulance. The surgeon seemed surprised to find me alive. Two orderlies pushed my gurney, almost at a full run, towards an operating room.

The surgeon jogged alongside. "If I have to replace your valve, what kind do you want?"

I had no idea how to answer. I wanted to say, *How about you put in one that works, Doc?* But after a few seconds of thought, I said, "If I were your brother, what kind would you use?"

"Synthetic."

"There you go."

They prepped me for surgery. I had very little time before they would put me under, but in those few minutes I was able to see Patti and my brother-in-law, Matt.

Somehow, they had beat the ambulance coming from Apple Valley. First of all, next time they should let me drive. Second, when Patti walked into my hospital room, she was surprised to find me at peace. She'd later say it was like I was glowing.

My aorta had split. They were about to open my chest and stop my heart for a surgery which would last fourteen hours. But, facing this, I had leaned into the light of Christ.

I had totally accepted God's plan, whatever it was going to be.

The surgery was a success, but it left me in a coma for five days. After I finally woke up, I still faced a long road of recovery. I'd spend the next couple of months in and out of the hospital undergoing all kinds of procedures. For a long time, almost every visiting surgeon or doctor would duck into my room looking defeated, like they were dragging a hundred pound weight behind them. They clearly didn't expect me to make it.

But Jesus walked with me and my family with every step. I had some bad days but I was always calm, knowing God's got me and the people I love.

The peace of Christ is an amazing thing. No matter where I was, no matter the chaos going on around me, I could feel it inside me.

And it radiated out. His peace touched nurses, doctors, family, friends - absolutely everyone who came to visit.

Fifteen

I spent the first fifty years of my life in darkness. Instead of hope, I gave off hurt. Instead of peace, I spread chaos.

At its worst, towards the end, I had drugs and cash - and people who would do anything to gain my favor.

I had women but no love. I had power but no joy. I had money but no light.

I knew nothing but darkness.

And the darkness spread. In the year before my arrest, it became clear I was being watched. The cops would sit outside my house. They'd pick me up for anything. One time I was stopped for doing one mile per hour over the speed limit.

I knew the end was coming, and I could have walked away. I could have done a thousand things differently, but I didn't know how to change. I was so deep inside the darkness that prison seemed like the only way out.

Finally, they arrested me outside Perkins for selling that ounce of meth. It was a fairly serious charge, but it was my first offense, and they had nothing else. They had no proof of manufacturing. They didn't have the red phosphorous. They didn't have black iodine crystals. They didn't have any pills.

In jail, I immediately started playing the system. My plan was to get into Teen Challenge. I figured I'd serve out an easy year in treatment and get back on the street. I hired an expensive attorney to make it happen.

But on Monday night, a few weeks after I arrived, a guard called my name and ordered me to Screen Two. I sat in front of a little television and picked up the phone. A woman appeared. She had covered her face with her hands, and was sobbing so hard it took a moment to recognize her. When I did, my jaw dropped.

My ex-wife had come to visit.

She barely said hello before getting into it. My oldest son was in the same jail, she told me, one unit over.

Up to this point I'd been floating through the system. They threw me in jail, but it was nothing, barely a speed bump. They couldn't touch me.

But that moment - hearing my son's name on my ex-wife's lips - destroyed me.

He had moved home a few months earlier. He had wanted to spend more time with me after turning eighteen.

I tried to create a normal life around us, but I couldn't hide my criminal operation. I never involved him in any of it, but he saw the darkness.

And the darkness spread. After my arrest, another meth cook asked my son to buy black iodine crystals from a medical supplier. These crystals are one of the ingredients for manufacturing the drug. It was legal to buy, but they checked your license and put your name on a list. A meth cook couldn't buy too often, but we had an easy workaround. We'd pay some kid a few hundred bucks to buy it for us.

My son took the money and made the run. At the supplier, they scanned his license and sent it to the authorities. An alert went out that his father was in jail fighting drug charges. They immediately arrested him for conspiracy to manufacture methamphetamines.

My ex-wife told me he was facing up to 48 months.

I stared at her. By the time she was done, I could barely breathe. They had more on my son than they did on me.

In John 11:9-10, Jesus tells his disciples, "If anyone walks in the day, he does not stumble, because he sees the light of this world. But if anyone walks in the night, he stumbles, because the light is not in him."

I was walking in the night. The light was not in me so I brought darkness with me wherever I went. It spread out from my life and touched everyone around me. It affected my parents. It affected my friends.

It affected my son.

I was responsible. I was a lot of things at that point in my life, most of them bad, but I was never a punk. I told my ex-wife to tell Brandon to keep his mouth shut and I would take care of everything.

The next morning I sat with my attorney in a windowless room.

"Listen," I said, "I want all charges on my son dismissed. I want him out of jail this afternoon. And I want all investigations on my house to stop right there."

He frowned at me and shook his head.

"To do all that," I said, "what will I need to plead to?"

He disappeared for ten minutes and came back with an offer: 110 months.

The day before I had been expecting to skip prison altogether and hang out at a treatment center. Now I was facing almost ten years, but I signed the plea. Even in the heart of darkness I wasn't going to let my son do time for my mistakes.

He walked free and I went to prison, but this is what darkness does. It fills your life with chaos. It spreads to those you love. And it follows you wherever you go. Prison was hell, but so was my life outside of prison. Behind bars or in my garage, it didn't matter; I was just stumbling through the night.

When you're in the darkness, it is with you wherever you are. When you're in the darkness, it touches the people around you.

But when you're in Christ, His light is with you wherever you are. When you're in Christ, His light touches the people around you.

Before I knew Jesus, I could possess everything the world had to offer and still be miserable.

Jesus brought me more joy than I can ever explain. After I gave my life to him, I could be in a hospital room, face to face with death, and still be at peace.

Don't be like me. It took me fifty years to give my life to Jesus.

If you are living in darkness, you don't need to wait. Right now, Jesus is offering you His light, His love, His peace.

I know it's hard. You have to surrender. You have to get on your knees and give up control of your life.

But now is the time.

God is light. In Him there is no darkness at all.

Turn to Jesus. And turn to the light.

GOD
SURPRISES

Sixteen

JOHN called me a week before the event.

"Hey Dennis," he said, "I need a bio from you. Could you put together a couple sentences explaining why men should pay to hear your story?"

I had been invited to be the keynote presenter for a men's conference at New River Assemblies of God in Red Wing, Minnesota. I had never done anything like it before.

"Um..." I said. "Let me get back to you on that."

Three days later my phone rang. It was John.

"Do you have something for me?"

"John," I told him, "for the life of me I can't figure out why anybody would want to come listen to me speak."

This wasn't false modesty. I had no business giving a talk at a men's conference. I was no public speaker. A few years earlier I wouldn't have even thought of doing such a thing.

But after months of heart surgeries and hospital stays, something had changed. I experienced the peace of Christ so deeply through a difficult period that I came out of it hungry to serve.

One night while I was still recovering at home, I went to

worship at River Valley Church. I was in rough shape and Pam Johnson (she and her husband Mark Johnson are both pastors) stopped me on my way out.

"Dennis..." She took in my sunken cheeks and gray skin. "Are you ever going to be able to work construction again?"

I had been struggling with that question myself. In the moment I wasn't sure if I'd make the walk to the car, much less run a backhoe. I shrugged and answered honestly.

"I don't know."

"Well," she said, "the ministry you do with these men... I always kind of thought of you as a pastor."

The question flipped a switch. The Holy Spirit started stirring things around inside my head.

Almost every week someone would stop me in church and ask me to talk to their brother or father or son. And when I wasn't laid up from my heart issues or working construction for twelve hours a day, I'd drive down to visit incarcerated men at Faribault prison.

I'd been doing this ministry for over a year, but, until Pam said something, I had never thought of myself as a pastor.

It wasn't long before I asked one of the pastors at church how to get started. He pointed me to The Berean School of the Bible. They offered nine classes, he explained, which ran $100 a piece.

I was growing more sure Jesus was calling me to ministry. But I wasn't sure about the price tag.

Patti was a stay-at-home mom. I was on temporary disability which didn't quite cover our mortgage. I had insurance but we still had a $6000 deductible.

All told, we had about $150 dollars in the bank.

I went home and bought the first course. Then I told Patti. She wasn't tickled.

But I felt strongly God was calling me to do this. I ran my life for the first forty-some years and it handed me a 110 month prison sentence. It was time to let God run it for awhile.

I told Patti, "I feel this is what I need to be doing. If this is God, he'll take care of the money part."

She looked skeptical.

"And if it's not God, we'll eat at your mom and dad's for the month."

We went back and forth about it for the rest of the night, then went to bed without a resolution. The next day we went to visit Patti's sister, Sarah, and her husband, Tony.

As we talked, I told them about these Bible courses. I didn't say a word about the cost or our empty bank account.

Tony barely let me finish my sentence. "Dennis," he said, "let Sarah and I bless you on this. Let us pay for your courses."

I stammered out some kind of response, and he immediately wrote out a check for all the courses, including the one I had paid for the night before.

Patti and I looked at each other. She was crying. I started crying.

When I could catch my breath, I said, "I think God spoke."

Seventeen

In 2016, I became a credentialed pastor.

Around the same time, I grew healthy enough to go back to my construction job. During the day, I'd work the backhoe, then on nights and weekends I'd minister to men. I focused on men who were like me - those in prison or in the grip of addiction.

It was overwhelming. I lost out on time with my wife and family. Construction punished my body. Still, I figured I was doing what God wanted of me. I figured I had it under control.

But then Charley called me.

I knew Charley from the years before I went to prison. He was one of the first people I met after I lost my family. He sold me drugs and introduced me to his crew. They were serious, violent men.

For awhile, I gladly followed Charley deeper into the dark world of addiction. Eventually, however, he was arrested for the sale and possession of drugs. He went to jail, and then prison, and we lost contact.

One night he lay in his cell. As he stared at the brick wall, the Holy Spirit pushed him to take an honest look at himself. He considered his life, what he'd done. He thought about his future, what he had to look forward to when he got out.

It was all pain.

Alone in his cell, he sank his knees to the cement and his elbows to the cot. There, he cried out to God. "Help me. I don't know what to do, and I need help."

Immediately, he knew he wasn't alone. Jesus showed up for him that night, and Charley was saved.

A few months later, in my own prison a hundred miles away, a friend grabbed my arm.

"Did you hear?" He smirked. "Charley found Jesus."

"Charley? What is he trying to get out of it?"

We laughed, but it was no joke. When Charley finished his stint, he immediately joined up with New River Assemblies of God in Red Wing.

Years passed. I finished my own time in prison. Charley and I had no contact as I lived with my dad, as I went back to work in construction, or as I dated Patti.

For almost a decade, Charley and I didn't talk. Then, three days after I gave my life to Christ, I pulled up at a job site. I started preparing for the day like any other. Behind me, I heard the door of a pickup truck thump and turned without thinking.

It was Charley, there to install a sprinkler system.

I leapt up and started for him with a huge smile on my face. Later, Charley would tell me he saw me coming and thought, "Well, this is either going to be really good or really bad."

It only took three days before God connected me to Charley. This is what God does; He brings people together to do His work. And after I became a pastor, it was Charley who invited me to speak at the men's conference at his church.

I had no idea why anyone would want to listen to me. I was no preacher. I became a pastor to minister - mostly one on one - to men in prison and in the darkness of addiction.

Still, I was done making my own decisions.

I said yes.

Charley never lost contact with his old crew. He'd watch the roster at the Goodhue county jail and visit anyone we used to run with. He'd sit with these men and tell them about a better way - through Jesus.

Before the conference, Charley called a couple of these guys and told them they should come listen to me.

One was my old friend Kevin (he went by Opie when he was in the gang). He came into church wearing skull rings on his fingers. Tattoos crawled up his neck and over his temple. He had cleaned himself up, but was still a biker.

We ate together before the conference. As we were finishing, he stared me down.

"Dennis, I'm going to sit in the front row. You better tell it like it was or I'm going to call you on it."

I laughed, but he wasn't kidding. When I got up there, I told it like it was.

But this was my first time telling my story in front of an audience. I had written everything down ahead of time, but I lost my place after only a few minutes.

I stumbled through a sentence, about fifty men watching me. "Shoot," I said, then finally admitted, "I'm lost."

The pastor of the church - Pastor Tom - yelled out, "Throw those notes away! You don't need them!"

He was right. I looked away from the pieces of paper, said a quiet prayer, and simply told my story.

The men listened.

In the end, I had no intention of doing an altar call. But God's intentions are often different than ours. So, without really meaning to, I invited the men to close their eyes.

"If you feel the Holy Spirit calling you to give your life to Christ today, raise up your hand."

Kevin's hand was the first one up.

Eighteen

MY ministry has never been about the masses. It's always about the one. And the one that night was Kevin.

After worship, I found him in the back, joking with some of the old crew.

I said, "Kevin, just think how powerful it would be if you and I spoke together. Or you, me and Charley."

Losing the smile, he spoke in his deep voice. "I don't do public speaking."

I had to laugh, because I had said the same thing to Charley not long before.

"Kevin," I said, "think if somebody came up to us fifteen years ago and said, 'Someday Dennis is going to be a pastor.' What would we have told him?"

He grinned. "He'd probably be a mound of dirt somewhere out in a field."

"That's right," I said. "So don't ever say never to God."

You are not God and neither am I. We only get to see bits and pieces, but God sees the whole thing. God has a plan for your life. And his plan is a lot bigger than yours. He will surprise you in ways you cannot imagine.

You just have to say, "Yes!" when he calls.

We haven't spoken together in front of an audience yet, but Kevin has started speaking in front of groups, leading AA meetings.

Never say never to God.

God Laughs

Nineteen

With two young boys at home and a demanding construction job, ministry was little more than a hobby.

I'd make the trip to visit Faribault prison on a Saturday, but only if I didn't have family obligations. I'd meet a struggling addict for lunch, but only if I could get away.

God kept telling me he had more for me to do, but I had no time. I had to be around for my wife and kids so the only thing that could go was work.

My heart surgeries forced me to slow down. I climbed off the backhoe every day in some kind of pain. Still, it was a good paycheck and I come from practical people. I couldn't imagine telling one of my sisters that I left construction for ministry. Why would anyone choose to spend time in a prison - unless they're getting paid? For my family - for most people - it simply didn't make sense.

Still, God kept nudging. Every day He'd get my attention in some different way, making it clear He had more for me to do. And every day I'd have to again explain to the Lord of the Universe all my reasons why I couldn't.

Months passed. God was patient with me for a time, but at

some point He had enough.

In early 2017, I went to see my cardiologist for an echo-cardiogram, which was like an ultrasound of my heart. After-wards, I sat calmly in her office. Every other visit, she had told me my heart looked fine and sent me on my way.

This time she frowned.

"Dennis, I want you to go to the university and get a coro-nary angiogram."

I didn't know what that was, but it didn't sound fun.

She told me they needed to insert a wire near my groin and run it up to my heart. There, they'd release a dye then take a series of pictures.

I sat back in my chair, my mind struggling to understand this information. I worked backwards - if I needed the test, then something must be wrong.

"Well," I finally said, "what's going on?"

"It looks like the grafts where they replaced the arteries around your heart are shrinking." A lump grew in my gut as she spoke. "It's very unusual, and I don't know why it's hap-pening. I'm sorry."

I stumbled out to my truck in a haze. For a long time I sat, my hands on the steering wheel, not moving.

When my aorta split, I had no time to think. I had no de-cisions to make. I dialed 911 and it all happened from there. I went along from moment to moment because if I didn't, I would die.

It wasn't easy, but it was simple.

This time, however, the hospital couldn't schedule this test for a few weeks, so I had to wait. And as I waited, I had time to think.

I went along with my life, but I couldn't get it out of my mind. I kept imagining the worst. I was sure the test would show my heart was failing and they would have to bust me open again. The idea terrified me. Physically, I never quite got my strength back from the last time they worked on my chest.

I didn't know if I could go through it again.

A few days before the procedure, I made a decision. If the test showed that I had to have another surgery on my heart, then - if I survived it - I'd finally listen to God. I would quit working construction and enter the ministry full time.

It would solve one problem. To my sisters, to my mom, to anyone who looked at me sideways for leaving a good construction job, I could use my heart as an excuse. I wouldn't be stepping away from a steady paycheck to do some touchy-feely thing. I would be retiring because my heart was no longer strong enough to handle the work.

Somehow, a weak heart sounded better in my head than a calling from God.

Twenty

I PUT on the gown. I followed the nurse's orders. I laid quietly as the doctor shot dye into my heart. I waited for the results.

Afterwards, the surgeon sat near my bed. "Dennis," she said, "I'm not sure what the cardiologist saw, but we think your arteries look awesome."

This was the best possible news. The grafts were holding up. I wouldn't have to face surgery. I should have rejoiced.

But I was ornery.

"Why did I have that test, then?" I grumbled. "It cost a lot of money."

The surgeon listened patiently.

"Well, Dennis, number one, your cardiologist wasn't the only one who looked at your EKG and CT scan. A number of doctors saw the results and they all made the same recommendation. Trust me, we wouldn't do this test without a reason. It is invasive and we never know how the heart is going to react. Patients have gone into cardiac arrest during this procedure."

She shook her head.

"We find a problem in over 90% of the patients who have

this test. Most have to have some kind of follow up surgery to fix something. You are the exception. This is great news. Your arteries look awesome. You're good to go."

I thanked her, then stared up at the ceiling after she left. Something was stirring in my mind and I wanted to figure it out before I moved from that hospital room. I can be a slow learner sometimes and it took awhile before it finally hit me. When it did, I started to laugh.

"Okay, God," I prayed, "Okay. I get it."

It happens throughout the Bible. With Moses, it was a bush on fire which refused to burn out (Exodus 3). With Peter, it was a net so full of fish they could barely haul it into the boat (Luke 5). With Abraham and Sarah, it was a pregnancy for a woman decades past her childbearing years (Genesis 18).

God loves to surprise those who follow him.

I would never compare myself to the heroes of the Bible, but it is still the same God who continues to act in our lives. The Holy Spirit is moving across this world, lifting up the followers of Jesus and calling them to service.

God told me to go into the ministry, but I wouldn't listen. He didn't swallow me up in a fish, thankfully, but he did get my attention with an angiogram.

Even after that, God didn't want me to use some medical condition as an excuse. He made sure my heart was fine, so that I had to be honest about it - to my family, my friends, and myself.

I got the message and, before I left the hospital, I made my decision.

I was going to quit a good, well-paying job. I wasn't retiring. I wasn't leaving because I had a bad heart. No, I had only one reason.

I needed to follow Jesus.

Twenty-one

GOD made it clear to me what I needed to do, but unfortunately He didn't tell my wife. That job He left to me.

It was winter; my company laid us off for the season, so I put it off by telling myself I had plenty of time. Besides, I had no idea where to begin. I didn't know anything about running a ministry, or raising funds, or creating a non-profit. None of those skills were required for operating a backhoe.

I moped around the house for a few days until our friend, Amy, knocked on my front door. She barely let me say hello before bursting into my house.

She started speaking so fast I could barely keep up. On Sunday, she told me, they had a ministry fair at her church. All kinds of people had booths filled with information about what they were doing for God.

She had walked around, inspired by all the good work being done. But one booth in particular caught her attention. Breakthrough Ministries, it said. They were doing some amazing work with the homeless population in the Twin Cities.

Dave, the executive director of Breakthrough Ministries, sat behind the table. He had an easy charisma and a passion for his work. After he shared with her about his own ministry, Dave said he was looking for other ministries to raise up under his umbrella.

My name immediately popped into her head but she dismissed it. I hadn't told anyone about my plans yet. As far as Amy knew, I was going to work construction for the rest of my life.

Amy moved on to the other booths, but for the rest of the day and into the week, my name and Dave's kept popping into her head.

Breakthrough Ministries has an office not far from Amy's work. Finally, on her way home one afternoon, Amy took a detour. She didn't understand it, but she thought it would help if she could talk to Dave again.

He was happy to see her. He was happy to talk about his ministry. As she sat there, it was like God was screaming in her ear.

An hour later she was in my living room.

"Dennis, you need to go talk to this guy."

After hearing her story, I had to laugh. God wasn't messing around. Clearly, I could not put this off any longer than I already had. The next day, I visited Dave's office. He lit up as I explained the Spirit's calling on my life.

He told me he wanted to raise up other ministries and he would love to help me get mine going under his umbrella. He also wanted to start a mentoring program alongside his homeless ministry and thought I'd be a good fit.

I left amazed at how God works. A few days earlier, I had known He wanted me to enter into ministry full time, but I had no idea how to start. Well, in one conversation, God made it pretty clear.

There was only one thing left to do.

I had to go home and tell my wife.

Twenty-two

MY wife is no fool. As soon as I asked her to sit down, she gave me a knowing look.

"Patti," I started, "I've got a few questions for you."

She raised an eyebrow. "Okay."

"Do you believe I'm a man of God doing the best I can?"

"Yes," she said.

"Do you believe men are my ministry? Men who are broken. Men who are struggling like I once did?"

"Yes," she said. "Absolutely. Your story calls for that."

I looked at her and said, "I only have one more question, then."

She stopped me. "Dennis, what about your job? We need the income. And what about the boys? Their activities... And insurance. With your heart stuff..." She went on, and each of her concerns was more valid than the last.

I listened to what she had to say. She was absolutely right. I had no idea where the money would be coming from, but I've always been more comfortable working things out as I go - flying by the seat of my pants. Patti was more comfortable having a steady plan. She needed security.

Still, I felt God calling me to this. I figured as long as I was breathing, somehow we'd have food to eat.

I let her finish. Only when she couldn't think of any other objections to add to the list, did I speak.

"Well, Patti..." I gave her my most charming smile. "I didn't ask my question yet."

She sighed.

"Do we trust God?"

"Of course, but..." and I could see she was revving herself up again.

"Whoa, whoa," I said. "It's a simple question. Yes or no. Not 'Yes, but...' or 'Yes, when...' There are no gray areas when it comes to trusting God. Either we do or we don't."

She studied the floor for a few long minutes. Then she raised her head and looked me straight in the eyes.

"Yes," she said. "Yes, we do."

"Patti, I want to quit my job and start ministry full time."

She couldn't help but laugh with me.

"All right, Dennis," she said. "Go for it."

We didn't know what the next day would bring. We didn't know how my family would react. We didn't know how we would pay our bills.

All we knew is the God who spoke to me in the restaurant when my brother-in-law asked about my soul is the same God who filled me with his peace in the minutes before they cracked open my chest is the same God who equipped his servants throughout the scriptures and history, and is the same God who would walk with us tomorrow and every step of the way.

God had called me to take his light into the darkness of prisons and drug addiction. I knew if I followed his call, I could trust him to take care of my family, my finances, and all the rest.

It has been scary and exciting. The journey hasn't been easy. We've stumbled along the way.

But God has been faithful every step.

A few weeks after our conversation, I called my boss and told him I wasn't coming back in the spring.

We had less than three hundred dollars in the bank when I entered full-time ministry.

Three years have passed since that day.

We have never missed a single bill.

GOD
SEEKS

Twenty-three

Breakthrough Ministries was great to me. Dave gave me an office. He offered me a conference room where I could mentor men.

I started working as soon as I could. I did my prison visits. I met men for lunch. I began raising some funds. My office even had a window I could stare out of and think deep thoughts.

One of the first times we met, Dave sat me down in his office and prayed over me. He asked Jesus that a name for my ministry might come. As he prayed, two words pushed aside every other thought in my head.

"All In," I said when he was done praying. "God's calling me to All In Ministries."

Jesus had made it clear from the start what He wanted me to do: work with broken men, one on one, and help them heal. He wanted me to find those men in the darkness and guide them to the light.

It was going well, but Dave understandably wanted me to be a part of Breakthrough. He wanted me to join him for meetings. A couple nights a week he had me serving at the shelter.

In those first months with Dave, I started to get a hitch in my spirit. I have a deep respect for Dave's ministry, but it felt like my ministry to the men in prison and the world of addiction was being pushed aside, and Breakthrough was taking over.

One morning I got down on my knees. I rested my elbows on the ottoman and closed my eyes. "God, I'm looking to serve you, here. What do you want me to do?"

God couldn't have been clearer. "I already told you," He said.

God had called Dave to Breakthrough Ministries - and he was doing great work - but God was calling me to something different.

I spoke with Dave later that morning. I thanked him for his help but explained how I had to leave.

I worried it would be a hard road. I'd have to get a board of directors, and hire a lawyer to apply for a 501c3, and start contacting donors. There was a lot of work in starting your own ministry.

But God blessed me. He put the right people in front of me right when I needed them. Within four weeks, I was ready to go.

From that point on, I've been able to dedicate each day to doing the job that God called me to do.

I go out to find the one in darkness.

And I try to bring him to the light.

Twenty-four

THE door slammed shut behind me. Somewhere, a guard eyeballed me through a camera. I was in a narrow hallway called a Sally-port. It had no air circulating and I smelled the sweat of the countless men who had stood there before me. My pockets were empty - I had to give everything up except for the cross hanging around my neck.

Finally, the door buzzed and I stepped into the visiting room. It was a large space with rows of hard plastic chairs facing each other, each row about three or four feet apart. Wives, parents, and children sat scattered, talking to their loved one and filling the room with chatter.

The man I was visiting stood waiting in the designated spot - a square of carpet monitored by guards where visitors and inmates were allowed brief contact. I grabbed him for a quick hug and we sat down.

This man was always a hard visit, and for an hour he sat, staring down at his hands. He mostly gave one word responses to each of my questions. I filled the silence between us with empty blather.

It was exhausting.

His mom had reached out to me after he overdosed before going to prison. The first time I showed up he spent the hour trying to convince me he was innocent.

"I'm not a judge. I'm not the jury," I told him. "But I prefer if you don't lie to me."

I tried to meet his eye, tried to get him to hear me.

"I'm here as a pastor," I said, "because Jesus wants you in heaven just like anybody else. That's why I'm here."

I almost always leave that visit feeling drained. No matter how many times I make the drive, no matter what I say or how hard I pray, his world, his spirit, his future seems just as dark as if I hadn't shown up at all.

Still, in a few weeks I will hand over my keys and my wallet, and I will stand in the Sally-port again. I'll breathe in the stale air and experience an uncomfortable flashback. In 2006, I walked out of prison a free man. As my dad drove me away, I swore I'd never return.

It's a sign of God's sense of humor that he keeps sending me back.

But that's what I do. I'll sit with the inmate again and do my best to offer him hope.

And no matter how exhausted I feel when I leave, I'll head back a few weeks after that... and again and again. I'll only stop if he specifically asks me to.

I keep showing up because I've been in that darkness myself.

I know how it feels.

This ministry is not easy. There are not a lot of high points, but this is the job God has called me to do. Show up in the prison. Show up in the halfway house. Show up in the restaurant. Sit with the man struggling in the darkness. And shine the light of Christ into his life.

Twenty-five

THE Men's Advance conference at Lake Geneva Christian Center in Alexandria, Minnesota is a great event. I always enjoyed it.

But they put my table right next to Vincent Miller.

Vincent Miller is an amazing man. He's written ten books. He started the Resolute Program. He filled his table with hats and colorful brochures and cool stuff.

Next to his, my table looked bare.

Throughout the morning, men stopped by every few minutes to talk with him. These were good, honest Christian men, so most of them didn't stop at my table. They weren't looking for freedom from addiction or someone to visit them in prison.

I'll be honest, as the hours passed, I grew envious. Again, I love Vince. He's always encouraging me, and offering great ideas. But he was getting all the action. I even had a bowl of candy, but people would sample my candy and go back to talk to Vince. I tried to tell them, "Hey, that's my bait." But I may as well have been talking to fish for how they listened.

It was almost time for the first presentation. My candy sup-

ply was dwindling - along with my hopes. I had all but decided this would be my last year buying a table for the conference
when I saw a man walk through the front doors. It took me
a second look, but I recognized him. His name was Steve and
we had done time together. Last time I'd seen him he'd taken
the bottom bunk in the annex at Saint Cloud state prison.

Steve was the last person I expected to step through that
door. He noticed me about three seconds after I saw him, and
he hurried over with a big smile on his face. We hugged. He
told me he had been released from prison three days earlier
after an eighteen-year stretch. I was immediately in tears.

I showed him my table and told him about my ministry. He
was flabbergasted. He kept staring at me, shaking his head. He
couldn't believe how much I'd changed.

"Dennis," he said, "I wasn't going to come up here. All the
way I'm thinking, what am I doing?"

A man he didn't know had stopped at his halfway house
and invited everyone to the conference. Steve wasn't sure
what led him to do it, but an hour later he was in his car. As
he drove down the highway he kept thinking, "What am I doing? I'm not even Christian." He figured he wouldn't know
a single person. More than once he approached an exit and
almost convinced himself to turn around.

There were over 700 people at that conference. Steve
walked in a stranger, feeling intensely that he didn't belong.

The first person he saw was me.

As I said before: God brings people together. He makes
connections we would never expect or imagine.

But it gets even better.

The first presentation was starting so Steve went ahead
without me and found an empty seat in the auditorium. The
crowd filled in around him. After a couple of minutes, a man

shuffled into the empty chair to his left. Steve glanced over and was shocked. It was a man he had done federal time with twelve years earlier.

The Holy Spirit had prompted Steve to go to this conference and he'd argued the whole way, griping to God about how he wouldn't know anyone. Then the first two people Steve ran into were both guys he knew from prison. And both of them had turned their lives around.

This is what God does.

But it gets even better.

At lunch, he started chatting with someone who turned out to be the brother of a man who mentored Steve during his time between prison stints. As they were eating their sandwiches, this man offered him a job.

At that conference it was almost unfair. Jesus hit Steve alongside the head with old friends and a job offer. He brought the man to tears.

Steve had a profound encounter with the Holy Spirit. The cool thing about God is that I did too.

I had let myself get discouraged. I sat staring at my bare table with its disappearing candy and felt sorry for myself.

What God did for Steve was a reminder. I did not become a pastor to gain a huge following. I was at that conference for one person: Steve.

It's good we have preachers who can connect with stadiums full of people, but that's not my ministry. God did not call me to preach to the masses.

I'm called to help the one.

——— GOD ———
FORGIVES

Twenty-six

JORGE grew up in gangs. As a young adult, he embraced the life and it eventually led to twenty years in prison. But after he got out, he gave his life to Christ.

His faith gave him hope but he still struggled. As often happened, someone from his church knew me and thought it would be good if we connected.

We met for lunch at TGIFridays. Our server took our order with a huge smile and an excess of energy. In contrast, Jorge acted like it was an effort to raise his head.

I took out my Bible, and on a hunch I read Matthew 18:21-22, where Peter asks, "Lord, how many times shall I forgive my brother or sister who sins against me? Up to seven times?"

Jesus answers, "I tell you, not seven times, but seventy-seven times."

Jorge finally looked up at me.

"Dennis," he said. "I understand I need to forgive others, and I can do that all right. But..." He stopped to rub the top of his head. "But I'm having a real hard time forgiving myself."

They called me Otto-matic in prison. It was a play on my last name, but also because if you messed with me, it was automatic: I'd come after you and not stop until it was finished.

And I'd smile when I did it.

A few months into my stint, they transferred me from Hastings to St. Cloud where my new cellmate was a young black man. For the first week we didn't say a word to each other. We were in lockdown, so we spent twenty-three hours of every day sealed in a tiny cell together, pretending the other didn't exist.

One morning I went to take a shower. When I came back, I found my cellie waiting. He had removed his shirt, tied his shoes tight and was dancing around.

"I'm going to F- you up, old man."

I wasn't surprised. I hadn't been a model inmate in Hastings. I was a very racist person and kept getting into fights with members of black gangs. My actions had clearly followed me. This kid wanted to get some payback for his friends.

I wasn't interested in paying up.

It was an old school prison, three floors of cell after cell, closed in with bars. I stood in the hallway, watching him dance for a few seconds. I could have walked away or called for a guard, but neither of those options crossed my mind.

I was Ottomatic.

"Let's go, old man!"

I stepped into the cell, then slid the gate shut behind me until it locked. Now neither of us could get out. I let the young man make the first move but I made the second.

The fight did not last long. There was a lot of blood.

The point is: I enjoyed it. Fighting gave me a surge of adrenaline and a momentary release from my own pain. Ottomatic was who I was.

It only grew worse after that. I looked for violence wherever I could find it. It got to the point that a friend had to pull me aside. He stared me down until he was sure I was listening. This man - who was a hitman for the Mexican Mafia - told me I needed to settle down. Violence and death was his livelihood, but after watching my behavior, he worried I was losing control.

Sitting in the TGIFriday with Jorge nearly ten years later, I understood exactly what he was saying. Like him, I'd given my life to Christ, but was - and am still - haunted by the things I had done. I had spent plenty of nights staring up at the cracks in the ceiling and asking the same question.

How do I forgive myself?

No answers would come. I had nothing figured out.

I was just as lost as Jorge, so I stared at him without any idea of what to say. It might have ended there, except it wasn't just the two of us at that table.

"I'm having a real hard time forgiving myself," Jorge said.

I had nothing, but the Holy Spirit was with us. And He spoke through me.

"Then don't."

Jorge looked at me, puzzled. "What the heck does that mean?"

I rested my hand on the Bible. "Show me in here where Jesus says to forgive yourself. You can't, because he never says it."

His eyes widened. "Are you for real?"

I nodded. "You know why he never says it? Because that's his job. Jesus does the forgiving. You need to get out of the way and let him do his job."

He was quiet for a long moment. Then he said, "You sure

that's not in the Bible?"

At that point I had to laugh. "You know, Jorge, it just came to me as I said it. Honestly, I'm hoping it was the Holy Spirit because I'm not really sure."

He smiled but I could tell he was thinking hard about it.

A week later, we met again for lunch, and he burst into the restaurant.

"Dennis," he said. He eyes were brighter and his words came quicker than the week before. "I looked all over. I put the words in the concordance. I googled it. You were right. Jesus never said to forgive yourself."

Of course, I shrugged and sat back in my chair. Acting all smart, I said, "I told you that last week."

We laughed, but we knew it was the Holy Spirit. Jesus had spoken through me in order to tell Jorge something we both needed to hear.

In Matthew 18, after Jesus tells Peter to forgive seventy-seven times, he tells a parable about a king who wanted to settle his accounts. The king calls in a servant who owes a lot of gold - thousands of bags worth. It would be millions - maybe billions - of dollars today, an impossible amount of money. The servant can't pay it, so the king orders him and his wife and children to be sold into slavery.

Hearing this, the servant falls on his knees and begs the king for more time.

The king has mercy. He doesn't just give the man an extension - he cancels the full debt (Matthew 18:23-27).

Jorge and I - and those like us - also owed an impossible debt because of our past. We stole. We sold drugs. We hurt people.

We were not nice guys.

There is no way we could ever make up for what we have

done. It is too much for us to repay.

In the parable, the servant didn't fix the problem himself. He didn't scrounge around, collecting funds. No, he went to the king for mercy.

And the king forgave his debt.

We have to do the same. We can't forgive ourselves. The debt is too steep.

We have to go to the King. Forgiveness is Jesus' job.

A few days after talking to Jorge, I sat down with my friend, George Fraser. He has a radio show in Minneapolis called Real Recovery Radio in which he talks openly about his struggles with addiction.

After I told him what I said to Jorge, George went quiet. Then he said to me, "You don't have a clue what you just did, do you?"

I shook my head. I was new to being a pastor, and worried I'd said the wrong thing or misunderstood the scripture.

"I have been struggling with this for years," George said. "I needed to hear that."

If you are anything like Jorge, George or me, then you need to hear it too. You can't forgive yourself. It's not possible and it's not biblical. So get out of the way and let Jesus do his job.

Twenty-seven

I KNOW I've been forgiven, but sometimes when I think about what I've done, it seems crazy God would want me to be a pastor. There has to be better people out there, people with cleaner resumes.

But God has never worked that way.

In Acts 9, a man named Saul was traveling towards Damascus to kill Christians. He wasn't the man to throw the stones. He didn't like getting his hands dirty. Instead, he was going to stand in the back and rile up the crowd to commit murder.

But before Saul could get there, Jesus blinded him on the road and threw him off his horse.

"Saul, Saul," Jesus said. "Why are you persecuting me?"

Saul repented and gave his life to Christ. And then a second miracle happened. Saul, who now went by Paul, became a preacher. He started traveling around from city to city, preaching about Jesus to anyone who would listen.

This man, who had persecuted Christians for years, became the greatest evangelist the world has known.

And this is how God works. He takes broken people and

uses them for his glory. He calls the unqualified and guides them with his Holy Spirit to do his work.

Years before I went to prison, before I became a meth cook, before I lost my family, before my divorce, I went through a time when I thought I had life figured out. I had a good job. I owned a house in a small town with my first wife. I was a captain in the fire department. I was respected in the community.

I was also growing marijuana in my basement and doing serious drugs on the weekends, but I didn't think much about any of that. It didn't seem serious. I figured I was a good guy, just having a little fun.

One afternoon I was pruning my pot plants in the basement, pulling off the leaves so they bud out. I heard a knock on the door so I climbed the stairs to find two older men from town on my front step. They asked if they could come inside.

We sat at my kitchen table. After a little small talk, they told me how the town was run. A couple of families made most of the decisions. We had members who had been on council for thirty years.

"We need some new blood around here," one of them said. "We need someone who's not related to everyone - and someone who will speak their mind." He pointed at me. "We need someone like you."

I sat back in my chair, nodding along with them. My heart filled with pride, and I thought, *Yeah, this town does need a council member like me.* Then I scraped some marijuana resin off my fingers.

I thought I was a good guy. I thought I was ready for leadership. I'd not only run for city council, I'd eventually become mayor for two terms. Those two older men looked at the life I showed the world and chose me for leadership. My life was rotten in the center, but outward things made me think I was qualified.

If God called people to ministry in the same way then I'd still be working construction. But God looks at the heart.

These days, I know I'm unqualified. I know I am broken. I know I am just as messed up - if not more - than the next guy. I am the last person Jesus should call to be a pastor.

But I also know it's not my job to decide who goes into ministry. That's God's job.

I know the things I've done and I will never forgive myself for them. But it's not my job to forgive myself. That's God's job.

The Apostle Paul was never addicted to meth, but before Jesus knocked him off his horse, he was probably addicted to power. He seemed to have a lust for violence. He was certainly the last man any person would have chosen to be a Christian preacher.

But Jesus forgave him.

And Jesus chose him.

And Jesus made him uniquely qualified to do the work he had been called to do.

I'm no Paul, but I've found myself to be uniquely qualified for the work the Holy Spirit has called me to do.

God has sent me to bring the light of Jesus into the dark world of prison and addiction. These men are willing to listen to me because I know what it's like. I know how they feel. I know what they think when they go to bed at night.

I am brutally honest with them. I often say, "I'm no baker. I don't sugarcoat anything." I tell them the hard truth, but I do it without judgement - because I know I am as broken as they are. I know I've been forgiven just as big of a debt.

Even when they relapse, I don't judge. The world of addiction is difficult to escape. Many of the men fall away, but when they do, they know my door is always open. They know they can come back at any time.

Because I've been there.

When they return, all I tell them is to fall forward. As they come back to sobriety, they should learn from the experience. Their relapse didn't happen in an hour or a day. No, they had been planning it for a long time.

I ask them to look back over the last few months, and figure out where it started. What was going on in their life? What were they feeling in their heart? What was happening in their head? I want them to learn so the next time they experience these feelings and thoughts, they can make adjustments.

Fall forward. Relapse is a learning experience, not a damnation experience.

I know this because I've lived it. I can minister to these men because I've been where they are.

I've been in the same darkness.

Now, by the grace of God, He is using me to spread the light.

In 1 Timothy 1:15, the Apostle Paul writes, "Here is a trustworthy saying that deserves full acceptance: Christ Jesus came into the world to save sinners - of whom I am the worst."

Paul called himself the worst of all sinners, but God forgave Paul and used him to spread the gospel through the world.

There is no sin too big. There is no past too ugly. There is no one too broken. You may not be able to forgive yourself but God can - and will.

But be careful. After that, He'll put you to work.

GOD —
FREES

Twenty-eight

AFTER a few weeks of class, Chris started getting into it. He'd lean forward in his chair to watch the videos. He'd be the first to talk during the discussion.

One week, however, a couple of guys from his gang showed up in prison. They were separated into different pods so decided to use my class - The Authentic Manhood 33 Series - as a place of contact.

The first five minutes were okay. I let them talk as I walked around the room, greeting the men and shaking their hands.

Eventually I said, "Okay guys, time for the DVD." Most nights they'd all quiet down. But Chris and his crew kept talking.

I took a deep breath, tried to settle myself, but I could feel a touch of the old Otto-matic rising into my chest.

Calmly, I raised the volume on the TV. On the screen, the sound bar went up and up, but they only grew louder with it.

My muscles tightened. My fists clenched. Finally, I lost it. "Hey!" I barked. "Keep it down! You're being very disrespectful."

It wasn't what I said as much as how I said it. For a moment

I was ready to throw down with all three of them.

But they grew quiet, and I sat back, angry more with myself than anyone. I had been working on my temper and it had frustrated me to have lost it again. When it was time for the discussion, Chris participated, but his new friends sat silently. They leaned back, arms crossed, eyeballing me.

It made the rest of the class tense. I knew if one of them came at me the other two - including Chris - would have to follow. Things would turn ugly for everyone.

But the discussion ended and nothing had happened. All three of the men left without any trouble.

Next week Chris came back alone.

After greeting him, I asked, "Where are your friends?"

Another man behind me shouted, "You hollered last week and scared them."

"About that..." I shook my head. "I shouldn't have lost my temper."

Chris said, "Dennis, don't think twice about it. As soon as you spoke up I knew we were wrong."

I appreciated that. But when the class had gathered, I felt like I had to say something.

"Listen," I said, "I know from experience that nobody is guaranteed the next breath. A couple years ago my aorta blew out when I was putting on my socks. This might be it. This next hour. This moment. Tonight, any one of you could be walking back to your pod and drop over dead."

I had their attention.

"Right here might be the only chance you have to know Jesus. Your only chance to give your life to Jesus. And if you don't because a couple guys have some catching up to do..."

I shook my head.

"I can't allow that to happen. Because this is life or death.

It really is. Now, I should have done it without anger. That's on me, and I'm sorry about that. But what we are doing here is life or death."

Twenty-nine

MANY of the inmates who attend my class don't know their fathers, so they don't have any good models of what it means to be a man.

When do you become a man? After your first beer? Your first cigarette? The first time you have sex?

We don't know, I tell them. There is no manual.

Except, of course, there is. The Bible was written thousands of years ago but it is still the best guide for what it means to be a man. I take the class through the scriptures, and we talk about these things. We talk about fathers and sons. We talk about work and respect. We talk about how to live as men in a hard world. I don't start with all the answers, but we figure it out together, with it all centering on Jesus.

Those men show up without a lot of hope. Most of them have done bad things to be there. Many of them have months, even years of prison ahead of them. It's a tough road, but I know they can be the men God created them to be. It's the reason I show up every week: I believe they can change.

I know it's possible because I have been exactly where those men are. I sat in my own prison cell, thinking I was tough and smart, thinking I didn't need anybody. I figured only the weak and foolish would turn to Jesus.

I was walking a dark path. And it didn't end even when they released me from prison. I simply brought the darkness with me. My relationship with my father helped, but I was still trapped in that old way of thinking. I continued to follow a road which led only towards death.

Six months after I was saved, I was baptized. Pastor Anthony plunged me under the water. When I came up he looked straight at me.

"Dennis, that old man is dead."

He shook my hand, gave me a hug and said it again.

"That man is dead."

Jesus changed me. I had been dead, but now I am alive.

I truly believe the men who come to my class can have a brand new life just like mine.

God has been good to me. Since quitting my job for one that raises a fraction of the income, somehow Patti and I are able to tithe more, pay our bills and still have some left over to do fun things as a family.

I've been blessed, but it's not the material things that matter. When I say they can have a life like mine, I'm talking about Life - meaning the joy and peace that come from knowing Christ.

I have joy and peace - and a loving family and some material possessions - because that old man is dead. Jesus gave me a new life.

The men who come to my class can have one too.

It won't be easy. I know this as well as anyone. These men need to draw the line in the sand. They need to stand up to the darkness inside and around them and say, "Enough." It is a part of what it means to be a man. It is a part of giving our lives to Christ.

Before King David was the greatest king of Israel he was the smallest of his brothers. Still, when the Philistine, Goliath, threatened the Israelite army, David trusted God and went out to fight the giant.

Goliath was huge. Shoulders like a beast. Legs like tree trunks. He had a lot of body to aim at, but David aimed high. He went after the smallest target: the giant's head.

David was a good shot, but there was no way he would make it on his own. Only with God's help did he kill the enemy (1 Samuel 17).

The acronym for All In Ministries is AIM. I often tell the men I work with: Aim high. Don't listen to what the world tells you. Listen to God.

These men I visit have been told over and over again that they'll never amount to anything. They'll always be a troublemaker. They'll always be a drug addict or a drunk.

Everyone around David told him he was a fool. He'd never make it off the battlefield. He'd never beat the giant.

David ignored those voices. He listened to God, and aimed high.

Same as I tell the men. They need to stop listening to those voices. They need to aim high.

Growing up, I imagined Jesus to be passive. I pictured him being barely there, someone who'd fade into the background if you weren't looking right at him.

But that's not Jesus.

Jesus called the religious leaders a brood of vipers (Matthew 12:34). He knocked over tables in the temple (Matthew 21:12-17). He said three words, "I am he!" And it knocked a battalion of soldiers to the ground (John 18:6).

I tell the men this is what they need to do. Aim high. Aim to be like Jesus. Stand strong. Assert yourself and say, "Enough!"

The world of addiction is a tough world to live in and a tougher world to leave. Most of the men I work with haven't made it out.

At times it can weigh on me. When a young man I've been working with for months stops calling and falls off my radar, I know what happened. It feels like the darkness has won, and it's easy for me to get down about it.

But I trust in the light. I believe we only see a small piece of the whole picture.

So to the men who have relapsed, to the families who loves them, and to any of you who are struggling in the darkness right now, I have a final word:

There is always hope. My door is always open. I won't judge. I won't condemn. When you're ready, let me know.

There is always hope. Even if I never hear from a person again I believe the Holy Spirit is working in their life. I may not get to see it, but someday something is going to stick with them and it will click.

There is always hope. The dark world of drug addiction has a powerful hold, but you can break free. I have been with men as they see the light of Jesus and have been blessed to walk with them through those first moments of joy. It can happen for you or the person you love.

And, finally, there is always hope. In the end, this is God's work. And God shines the light in the darkness and the darkness will never overcome it.

Epilogue

When I started All In Ministries in the spring of 2017, I had a vision for what it would be. I thought I had big dreams - but God's dreams were bigger. I never imagined we would be where we are today.

I work through the Dakota County jail systems and Stillwater Prison. I mentor with the Goodhue County Drug court. I visit men at halfway houses, restaurants, coffee shops and through phone calls and texts.

I've worked to bring Jesus into these men's lives, but God had more for me to do.

I work with families. As I help men in their struggle with addiction, I walk with their moms and dads and siblings and friends.

I've worked to bring the light of Christ into these family systems, but God still had more for me to do.

I work with churches. I tell my story, pointing at what Jesus has done. I speak in public places, wherever I'm invited - even once at Apple Valley Public Schools - and tell them about the miracle of resurrection that happened in my life.

And God still had more for me to do. I lead a class in the

Goodhue County Jail system. Every week I sit down with men who are broken like me and together we talk about what it means to be a man.

God has filled my life with blessings. He's given me an amazing partner in Patti, a great family, and the best in-laws anyone could want. I now count Patti's father, Bob Strom, as one of my best friends.

God has been good to me and I am privileged to do his work. I know He'll surprise me tomorrow with something new, and I will do my best to do it. As long as I have breath in my body, I will work to share the light and joy of Jesus with everyone I meet.

Maybe today that will be you. If this book has touched you, reach out to me. If you or someone you love is struggling with an addiction, let me know. Send me an email. It doesn't matter where you live, I'll answer. I'll do my best to walk with you or your family member through the darkness into the light.

It's not an easy journey, but God is doing miracles every day. You can have your own resurrection story.

There is alway hope.

Contact Pastor Dennis:
PO Box 240602
Apple Valley, MN 55124
www.allinministries.org
Dennis@allinministries.org

An Invitation

With God we are making a difference. I write "we" because it's not me alone doing this. Partnering with All In Ministries through your prayers and finances makes us a team. It is us on the streets; in the jails, courts, churches, and schools; and with the families.

All In Ministries is a privately funded non-profit. It has a 501c3, and is fully recognized by the state of Minnesota.

If you have been touched by the story of the book, I invite you to support the ministry through prayer, words of encouragement or a financial gift.

Together we can touch the lives of so many with the love of Jesus.

Testimonials:

"All In Ministries has been instrumental in our journey. Issues of addiction, violence, weapons, incarceration and mental illness have had profound effects on our entire family, and Dennis has been a source of guidance and hope. He has counseled us. He has comforted us. He has taught us when to show tough love.

He has prayed with us. Molly and I would have felt lost and lonely without having Dennis by our side. I can never thank him enough for what he has done."

-Pat and Molly

"I was introduced to All In Ministries coming out of a very dark couple of years. I was at my lowest and needed someone who could understand the things I was going through. Dennis showed up and added something to my life that had been missing, and that was Christ. Without his wisdom and guidance I'm not sure I would have made it to this positive place in my life. I know that I can call him any time day or night for guidance through anything. His encouragement and tough love has helped me through all the court hearings and eventually helped me get a full time job. I can't thank Pastor Dennis or All In Ministries enough for everything they have done for me and the things they continue to do."

- Jesse

Contact Pastor Dennis:
PO Box 240602
Apple Valley, MN 55124
www.allinministries.org
Dennis@allinministries.org

I would like to close this book with a prayer written by my friend and mentor Roger Lane.

Dear Lord,

I pray that the reader of this book be blessed and encouraged by its content.

I pray for those who have had errors in judgment that have caused pain both in their own life and in the lives of others.

I pray that You will grant your peace, forgiveness and love from this day forward.

I pray that You inspire each reader to encourage others on their life journey to find God through Your son, Jesus Christ.

I pray this in Jesus' name. Amen.

Made in the USA
Monee, IL
05 April 2021